INSECT W⊙RLD
PRAYING MANTISES

SANDRA MARKLE

HUNGRY INSECT HEROES

◣ LERNER PUBLICATIONS COMPANY MINNEAPOLIS

FOR CURIOUS KIDS EVERYWHERE

ACKNOWLEDGMENTS
The author would like to thank Dr. David Yager, University of Maryland, for sharing his expertise and enthusiasm. The author would also like to thank Dr. Simon Pollard, Curator of Invertebrate Zoology at Canterbury Museum, Christchurch, New Zealand, for his help with the scientific name pronunciation guides. Finally, a special thanks to Skip Jeffery, who shared the effort and joy of creating this book.

Lerner Publications Company
A division of Lerner Publishing Group, Inc.
241 First Avenue North
Minneapolis, MN 55401

Website address: www.lernerbooks.com

Library of Congress Cataloging-in-Publication Data

Markle, Sandra.
    Praying mantises : hungry insect heroes / by Sandra Markle.
       p. cm. — (Insect world)
    Includes bibliographical references and index.
    ISBN 978–0–8225–7300–5 (lib. bdg. : alk. paper) 1. Praying mantis—Juvenile literature. I. Title.
    QL505.9.M35M37 2008
    595.7'27—dc22   2007025961

Manufactured in the United States of America
1 2 3 4 5 6 – DP – 13 12 11 10 09 08

CONTENTS

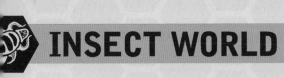
WELCOME TO THE WORLD OF INSECTS—

those animals nicknamed bugs. It truly is the insects' world. Scientists have discovered more than a million different kinds—more than any other kind of animal. And they are everywhere—even on the frozen continent of Antarctica.

So how can you tell if an animal is an insect? Compare this praying mantis to the millipede *(right)*? Both belong to a group of animals called arthropods (AR-throh-podz). The animals in this group share some traits. They have bodies divided into segments, jointed legs, and a stiff exoskeleton. This is a skeleton on the outside like a suit of armor. But one sure way to tell if an animal is an insect is to count its legs. All adult insects have six legs. They're the only animals in the world with six legs.

This book is about praying mantises. A praying mantis is a super hunter. Many of its prey are insect pests—insects that cause problems for people. By eating them, mantises become heroes.

MANTIS FACT

Like all insects, a praying mantis's body temperature rises and falls with the temperature around it. It must warm up to get the energy to hunt.

OUTSIDE AND INSIDE

ON THE OUTSIDE

Take a look at this female Chinese praying mantis. If you could touch it, its body would feel like tough plastic. Instead of having a hard, bony skeleton inside the way you do, an insect has an exoskeleton. This hard coat covers its whole body—even its eyes. The exoskeleton is made up of separate plates connected by stretchy tissue. That lets it bend and move. Check out the other key parts that all praying mantises share.

SPIRACLES:
These holes down the sides of the thorax and abdomen let air into and out of the body for breathing.

ABDOMEN

OVIPOSITOR:
The end of the female's abdomen. It is used for laying eggs.

WINGS: Mantises with wings have two pairs. A leathery front pair covers the hind pair. In some kinds of praying mantises, the females have very short wings or are wingless.

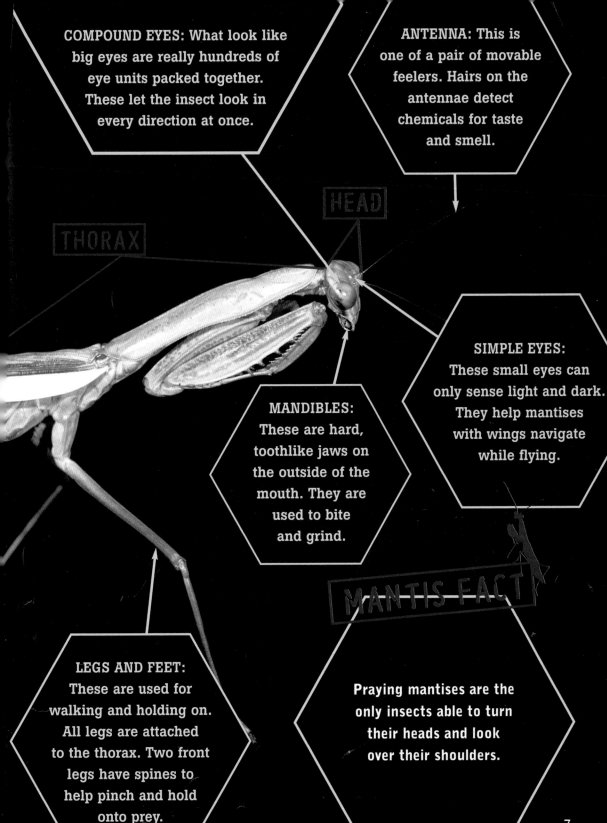

COMPOUND EYES: What look like big eyes are really hundreds of eye units packed together. These let the insect look in every direction at once.

ANTENNA: This is one of a pair of movable feelers. Hairs on the antennae detect chemicals for taste and smell.

HEAD

THORAX

SIMPLE EYES: These small eyes can only sense light and dark. They help mantises with wings navigate while flying.

MANDIBLES: These are hard, toothlike jaws on the outside of the mouth. They are used to bite and grind.

MANTIS FACT

LEGS AND FEET: These are used for walking and holding on. All legs are attached to the thorax. Two front legs have spines to help pinch and hold onto prey.

Praying mantises are the only insects able to turn their heads and look over their shoulders.

7

ON THE INSIDE

Now, look inside an adult female praying mantis.

CROP: The crop holds food before it moves on for further digestion.

INTESTINE (GUT): Digestion is completed here. Food nutrients pass into the body cavity to enter the blood and flow to all body parts.

HEART: This muscular tube pumps blood toward the head. Then the blood flows throughout the body.

SPERMATHECA: This sac stores sperm after mating.

RECTUM: Wastes collect here and pass out an opening called the anus.

OVARY: This body part produces eggs.

MALPIGHIAN TUBULES: These clean the blood and pass wastes to the intestine.

8

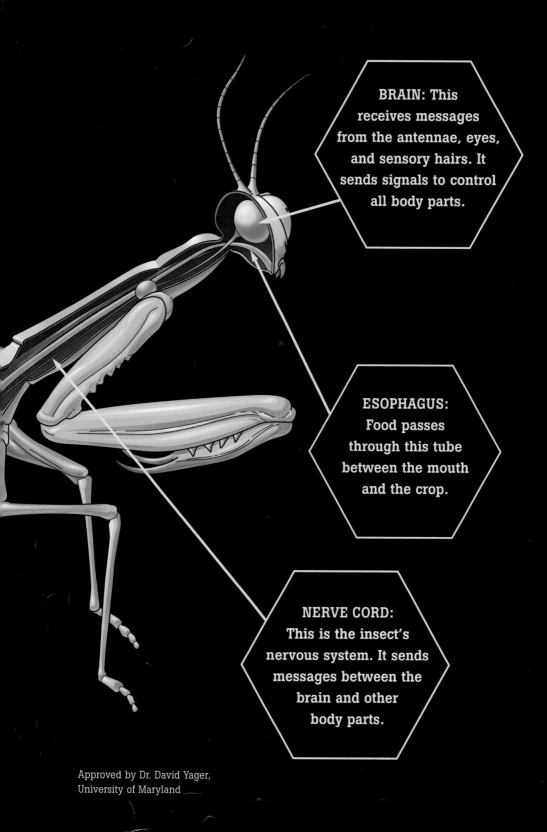

BRAIN: This receives messages from the antennae, eyes, and sensory hairs. It sends signals to control all body parts.

ESOPHAGUS: Food passes through this tube between the mouth and the crop.

NERVE CORD: This is the insect's nervous system. It sends messages between the brain and other body parts.

Approved by Dr. David Yager,
University of Maryland

BECOMING AN ADULT

Insect babies become adults in two ways: incomplete metamorphosis (me-teh-MOR-feh-sus) and complete metamorphosis. Metamorphosis means change. Praying mantises develop through incomplete metamorphosis. Their life includes three stages: egg, nymph, and adult. The nymphs look and act much like small adults. But nymphs can't reproduce. Compare these newly hatched Japanese mantis nymphs to the adult. The nymphs also won't be able to fly until they become adults.

IN COMPLETE METAMORPHOSIS, insects go through four stages: egg, larva, pupa, and adult. Each stage looks and behaves very differently.

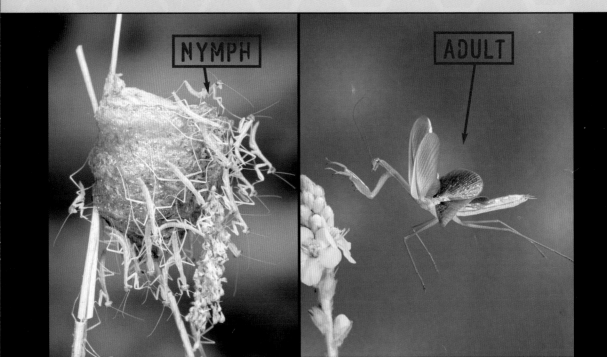

NYMPH

ADULT

The focus of a praying mantis's life is hunting. It's something it just naturally does, but it's built for this job. It is an ambush hunter, meaning it hides and waits for prey to come close. Its body is colored to blend in with the plants. It has big eyes to watch for prey. Its head is able to swivel to look in every direction. Once prey is within striking range, the mantis's front legs unfold in a flash. Snap! It grabs its prey and bites with sharp mandibles to make its kill. Most of the time, that prey is an insect that causes problems for people. So people are glad praying mantises are hungry hunters.

HATCHING NYMPHS

It's spring. The weather is warming up, and trees are starting to leaf out. On one branch, there is a European praying mantis egg case. All winter long, this hard, sturdy case kept the eggs inside it safe. It sheltered them from wind and rain. And it kept out egg-eating enemies, like spiders and ants. Now the nearly 300 praying mantis nymphs are hatching. One after the other, the mantis nymphs wiggle to the egg case's opening and escape.

MANTIS FACT

European praying mantis nymphs are only about 0.15 inch (0.4 centimeter) long. That's as tiny as an eyelash on your lower eyelid.

Like adult mantises, the nymphs have an exoskeleton, an armor coat. It was soft while the nymphs were inside their eggs, so they need to wait for this covering to harden. While they wait, they just naturally line up along the branch. Being tiny, they are hard for a predator to spot. They also stay close together at first. If a predator, such as a bird or spider, comes along, it will be safer for each little mantis to be part of a big group.

MANTIS FACT

Some kinds of praying mantises hatch in batches rather than all at once. This still lets them find safety in numbers.

BORN HUNGRY

Praying mantises have big appetites and sometimes eat other praying mantises. A nymph's first meal could be a brother or sister. But nymphs still need to watch out for other hungry hunters. Below, an assassin bug hunting for a meal catches a praying mantis nymph. The others hurry away.

One female mantis nymph crawls into a space among the leaves. Here, she stays hidden from predators. She is also hidden from the insect prey she's waiting to ambush. Her big eyes watch for anything that moves. Suddenly, she spots a flying insect. She tracks it until it comes close. Her front legs unfold with lightning speed. She snags her first meal.

MANTIS FACT

The European mantis has spines on its front legs. It drives these into its prey to hold on tight.

THE PERFECT DISGUISE

The female mantis nymph continues to hunt and eat. Soon she grows too big for her exoskeleton. She hangs upside down and molts, or sheds the armorlike covering. She already has a new protective coat underneath. This new coat is soft at first, though. She waits for it to harden. Then she starts hunting again.

Day after day, the female nymph sits on branches, waiting to ambush prey. Her shape and coloring camouflages her, or lets her blend in perfectly with her surroundings.

MANTIS FACT

Praying mantis nymphs go through six or seven molts in becoming adults.

After several more molts, the female nymph is no longer so tiny that she can't be easily seen. Instinct makes her add to her disguise. She clings to a branch with her claw-tipped feet, and she sways a little. This way, she blends in with the windblown leaves and twigs around her. Since she is bigger, she is able to catch bigger prey, like this caterpillar.

MANTIS FACT

Praying mantises have special chemical sensors on their feet to let them "taste" what they touch.

Later, she catches a cricket. The praying mantis kills its prey by eating it. So, holding her prey with her two front legs, the female nymph bites off a chunk. Then she bites off more. She catches another cricket. Catching one after another, she feeds herself and helps keep the cricket population under control.

MANTIS FACT

Healthy, hungry mantises have been recorded eating as many as 15 crickets a day.

OTHER DISGUISES

The European mantis's disguise is simple compared to some other mantises. For example, one from Guyana is called the moss mantis. The flaky bumps on its exoskeleton make it look like a moss-covered twig.

The body shape of this Malaysian rain forest praying mantis earned it the nickname orchid mantis. It stays still among orchid blooms and waits. A butterfly comes to sip the flower's nectar. The praying mantis reaches out fast. Gotcha! Its front legs snag its prey.

ADULT APPETITES

The European praying mantis nymph keeps on eating and growing. With each molt, her wings become bigger too. By the time she molts for the seventh time, she is an adult. This means her ovaries are ready to make eggs to produce young. Her wings are fully developed too. She's also the biggest she's ever been. She's able to catch larger prey than ever before.

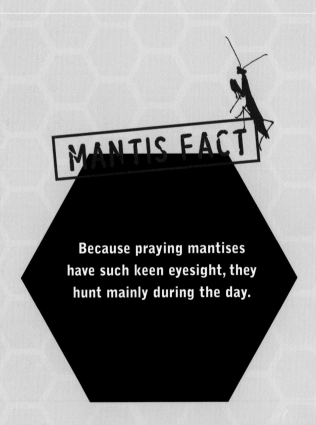

MANTIS FACT

Because praying mantises have such keen eyesight, they hunt mainly during the day.

SHED EXOSKELETON

Over the summer, the insect pests have grown bigger too. Every chance she gets, the female mantis catches large insects, like this grasshopper. For her, grabbing large prey means getting a bigger helping of food. But some of these prey insects, such as grasshoppers and crickets, damage growing fruits and vegetables. By eating them, the mantis also helps the people who raise and eat these food crops.

Between meals, the female praying mantis cleans herself. She pulls each antenna through her mouth. Then she cleans her body and her legs. She does this by instinct, but it helps her stay healthy. Her exoskeleton keeps her soft internal organs from drying out. By cleaning her exoskeleton, she removes bits of dirt that could scrape a hole in it.

Cleaning herself also helps her be a successful hunter. She wipes the gogglelike covering over her eyes. This keeps her vision sharp. Finally, she cleans her front legs. This keeps the spines ready to pinch and hold onto her next prey.

DEFENSES AGAINST ENEMIES

The adult female praying mantis is larger, so it's easier for predators to spot her. Suddenly, a bird swoops down. But before the bird gets close enough to attack, the mantis rears up on her walking legs. This makes her look even bigger. She also throws up her front legs in a threat display. She flutters her wings. They make a hissing sound. Startled, the bird swerves and flies away. The praying mantis's defensive action worked!

MANTIS FACT

Praying mantises can see movements as far as 60 feet (18 meters) away. That gives them time to react to prey and predators.

During the day, birds hunt flying praying mantises. At dusk, there are other winged enemies—bats. Bats hunt by giving off high-pitched sounds. Then they listen for echoes. They use the echoes to sense where objects and prey are. The European mantis has a special part of its thorax that acts like an ear. It can hear a bat's high-pitched sounds. When it detects the sounds, the mantis flaps fast and dives. Once the mantis is just above ground level, the bat swoops off after easier prey.

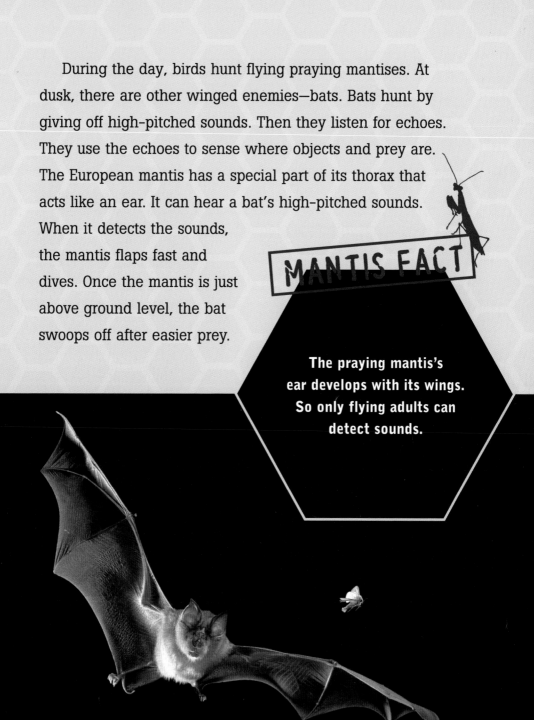

MANTIS FACT

The praying mantis's ear develops with its wings. So only flying adults can detect sounds.

THE CYCLE CONTINUES

Adult praying mantises may fly to find new places to hunt. They may fly to escape hunters. Male mantises also fly to search for a mate. The bigger, heavier female mantises stay put. To attract a mate, the female European praying mantis gives off special scents, called pheromones (FER-eh-mohnz). Males have sensory hairs on their antennae that let them track this scent.

MANTIS FACT

Since they don't fly to find mates, female mantises may absorb their flight muscles and use that food energy to produce eggs.

When the male European mantis gets close enough to spot the female, he lands nearby. Then he slowly walks toward her. All the while, he waves his antennae. The female waves her antennae too. Then both flex their abdomens. This is all part of their courtship. During mating, the male transfers a packet of sperm, reproductive cells, to the female's body. Then the male flies away. He will search for another mate. The sperm he deposited will be stored in the female's spermatheca until she's ready to lay her eggs.

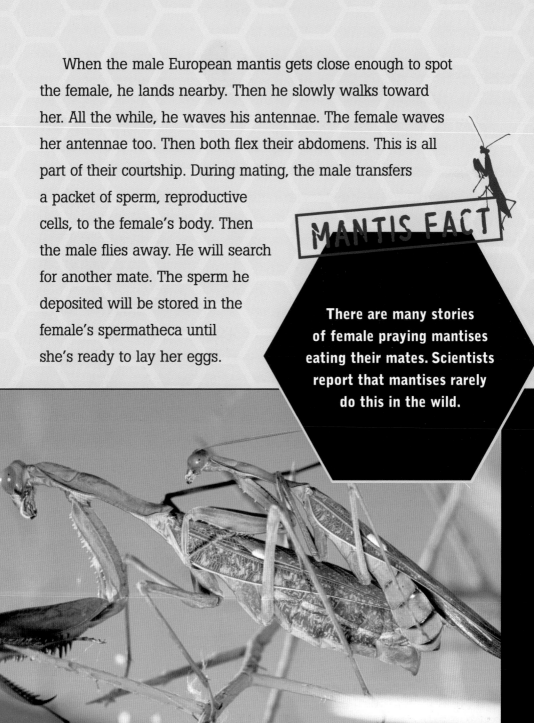

MANTIS FACT

There are many stories of female praying mantises eating their mates. Scientists report that mantises rarely do this in the wild.

When the female is ready to lay her eggs, she first makes the egg case. To do this, she presses her tail end against a tree branch. She releases a glob of jellylike material. At the same time, she twists her abdomen around and around. This way, she whips the jelly into foam. She deposits her eggs in the foam one at a time—nearly 300 eggs in all.

The foam dries quickly. In a short time, it's too hard for egg-eating predators, like spiders, to chew through. Its toast brown color blends in with the branch and hides it. The hardened foam also shields the eggs from wind, rain, and cold weather.

MANTIS FACT

It takes the female about 30 minutes to make her egg case and lay her eggs.

Praying mantises usually live a little less than a year. Once an adult male European mantis starts mating, it only lives about two to three weeks longer. The female European mantis lives on for about two months. During this time, she will produce two more egg cases. She keeps on hunting too. She needs lots of food energy to produce all those eggs.

At this time of the year, the praying mantis's hunting skills make her an even greater hero for humans. It's harvesttime. The more insects she eats, the fewer insects there are to damage crops.

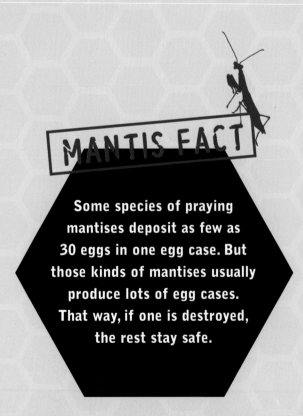

MANTIS FACT

Some species of praying mantises deposit as few as 30 eggs in one egg case. But those kinds of mantises usually produce lots of egg cases. That way, if one is destroyed, the rest stay safe.

Inside the egg case, the baby European praying mantises are already developing. But they won't hatch until the weather warms up in the spring. Lots of other young insects will hatch then too. The praying mantises will have lots of prey to catch. Throughout their lives, praying mantises help control the numbers of insects living around them. No wonder people are happy to have praying mantises as neighbors.

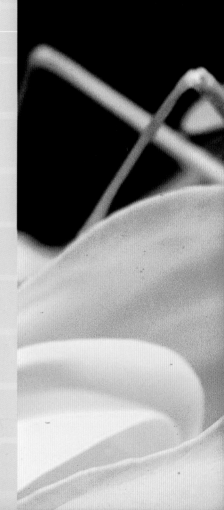

MANTISES AND OTHER INSECT HEROES

PRAYING MANTISES belong to a group, or order, of insects called Dictyoptera (dik-tee-OP-ter-ra). The name *mantis* comes from the Greek word for "prophet." The name refers to the way the insects look. Praying mantises hold their two front legs up as if in prayer. Of course, they are really just getting ready to ambush prey.

SCIENTISTS GROUP living and extinct animals with others that are similar. So praying mantises are classified this way:

> kingdom: Animalia
> phylum: Arthropoda
>   (ar-throh-POH-da)
> class: Insecta
> order: Dictyoptera

HELPFUL OR HARMFUL?
Praying mantises are mostly helpful because they eat insects that feed on farmers' crops or garden plants. They eat any insect they can catch, though. So praying mantises sometimes also eat helpful insects, like honeybees.

HOW BIG is a female European praying mantis? It can be up to 3 inches (7.6 cm) long.

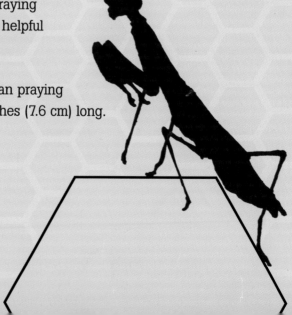

MORE INSECT HEROES

Other insects eat insect pests and are heroes too. Compare these insect hunters to praying mantises.

Ladybugs are valued because they eat aphids and scale insects, pests in gardens and orchards. After mating in the spring or early summer, the females lay their eggs close to an aphid colony. When the larvae hatch, they have food close by. Adult ladybugs hunt insect prey too. They bite the prey they catch to kill it.

Dragonflies are winged hunters that catch insect prey in the air. They are especially valued for eating lots of mosquitoes that might otherwise spread diseases. Dragonfly nymphs get rid of mosquitoes too. They live underwater in ponds, streams, and wetlands. There, they eat mosquito larvae, which also live in water.

Assassin Bugs catch and kill insect prey. They hunt when they are nymphs and when they are adults. Like praying mantises, they hide and ambush prey. But they don't bite to kill. They stab their prey with a long beak. Digestive juices flow in the prey insect, turning its insides into liquid. Then the assassin bug sucks up this liquid meal.

GLOSSARY

abdomen: the tail end of an insect. It contains the parts for digestion and reproduction.

adult: the final stage of an insect's life cycle

antennae: movable, jointed parts on the insect's head used for sensing

brain: receives messages from the antennae, eyes, and sensory hairs. It sends signals to control all body parts.

camouflage: to blend in with surroundings

complete metamorphosis: a process of development in which the young looks and behaves very differently from the adult. Stages include: egg, larva, pupa, and adult.

compound eyes: eyes that are really hundreds of eye units packed together. These let the insect look in every direction at once.

crop: area of the digestive system where food is held before it is passed on for further digestion

egg: a female reproductive cell; also the name given to the first stage of an insect's life cycle

esophagus (ee-SAH-feh-gus)**:** a tube through which food passes from the mouth to the crop, or stomach

exoskeleton: protective, skeleton-like covering on the outside of the body

head: the insect's body part that has the mouth, the brain, and the sensory organs, such as the eyes and the antennae, if there are any

heart: muscular tube that pumps blood

incomplete metamorphosis: a process of development in which the young look and behave much like a small adult except that they are unable to reproduce. Stages include: egg, nymph, and adult.

intestine (gut): digestion is completed here. Food nutrients pass into the body cavity to enter the blood and flow to all body parts.

larva: the stage between egg and pupa in complete metamorphosis

Malpighian (mal-PEE-gee-an) **tubules:** the organ that cleans the blood and passes wastes to the intestine

mandibles: the grinding mouthparts of an insect

molt: the process of an insect shedding its exoskeleton

nerve cord: the nervous system. It sends messages between the brain and other body parts

nymph: stage between egg and adult in incomplete metamorphosis

ovary (OH-vuh-ree): body part that produces eggs

ovipositor: tail end of the abdomen used to deposit eggs and make an egg case

pheromones: chemical scents given off as a form of communication

predator: an animal that is a hunter

prey: an animal that a predator catches to eat

pupa: stage between larva and adult in complete metamorphosis. At this stage, the larva's body structure and systems are completely changed into its adult form.

rectum: part of the digestive system where wastes collect before passing out of the body

simple eyes: eyes only able to sense light from dark

sperm: male reproductive cell

spermatheca (spur-muh-THEE-kuh): sac in female insects that stores sperm after mating

spiracles (SPIR-i-kehlz): holes down the sides of the thorax and abdomen. They let air into and out of the body for breathing.

thorax: the body part between the head and the abdomen

DIGGING DEEPER

To keep on investigating praying mantises, explore these books and online sites.

BOOKS

Hipp, Andrew. *Orchid Mantises*. New York: PowerKids Press, 2003. Investigate the lives of these beautifully camouflaged predators.

Scholl, Elizabeth J. *Praying Mantis*. Farmington Hills, MI: Thomson Gale, 2004. Explore this animal's life and its habitat.

Swanson, Diane. *Bug Bites: Insects Hunting Insects . . . and More!* North Vancouver: Whitecap Books, 2001. Compare the mantis's hunting style to that of other insect predators.

WEBSITES

Mantises Galore

http://www.emints.org/ethemes/resources/S00001413.shtml

Follow the links on this site to explore lots of other sites packed
with praying mantis information, photos, and activities.

Mantis Fun

http://www.maskedflowerimages.com/mantis.htm

Find the answers to fun questions, check out cool photos, and
solve a mantis word search puzzle at this action-packed site.

Praying Mantises

http://www.desertusa.com/mag00/dec/papr/mantis.html

After checking out the general mantis facts, follow the "More on
the Praying Mantis" link to learn myths about praying mantises
and about this insect's role in the food chain.

PRAYING MANTIS ACTIVITIES

STRIKE TIME

Scientists have studied the praying mantis's strike time. That's the time from when their front legs start to move until they catch their prey. It's approximately 70 milliseconds—so fast it's a blur. So how fast can you react to a moving target?

Work with a partner to find out. Have your partner hold a ruler with his or her fingers at the end with the highest number. Stand beside the ruler with your hand around but not touching the lowest number. Hold your thumb on the scale side of the ruler. Have your partner release the ruler without giving you any warning. As soon as you see the ruler move, grab it. This is much like the praying mantis spotting its prey. Your reaction time is recorded in inches or centimeters—the point on the ruler closest to your thumb when you stop the ruler. The lower the number is, the faster your reaction time.

A PRAYING GUEST

If you find an adult praying mantis in your yard or near your home, you could bring it home to watch. You'll need a container, such as a quart jar. Scoop in enough dirt to cover the bottom. Mist with water. Stick in a twig for the mantis to climb on. Once the mantis is inside the container, cover the top with clear wrap taped at the edges. Use a sharp pencil to poke a few airholes.

Now go hunting for other insects, such as large flies. An adult mantis is likely to eat at least two large flies a day. And mantises will only eat live prey. You'll have to lift the cover and slip these inside before resealing.

Watch the mantis for a day or two. Check out how it hunts. See how it eats. Then return the praying mantis to where you found it. Leave it to continue its life cycle.

INDEX

PHOTO ACKNOWLEDGMENTS

The images in this book are used with the permission of: © Dwight R. Kuhn, pp. 4, 6–7, 16, 47; © Stephen Dalton/Minden Pictures, pp. 5, 31, 41 (middle), 41 (bottom); © Bill Hauser/Independent Picture Service, pp. 8–9; © Kim Taylor/naturepl.com, p. 10 (both); © NHPA/Stephen Dalton, pp. 11, 17; © E.R. Degginger/Photo Researchers, Inc., p. 13; © Raymond Blythe/Oxford Scientific Films/Photolibrary, p. 15; © Armand Madrigal/Taxi/Getty Images, p. 19; © Francesco Tomasinelli/Natural Visions, pp. 21, 22–23; © Piotr Naskrecki/Minden Pictures, p. 24; © Michael & Patricia Fogden/Minden Pictures, p. 25; © Nancy Rotenberg/Animals Animals, p. 27; © Perennou Nuridsany/Photo Researchers, Inc., pp. 28, 29; © NHPA/Daniel Heuclin, pp. 30, 34; © Shin Yoshino/Minden Pictures, p. 32; © Carsten Peter/National Geographic/Getty Images, p. 33; © Millard H. Sharp/Photo Researchers, Inc., p. 35; © Cisca Castelijns/Foto Natura/Minden Pictures, p. 37; © Corbis/Photolibrary, pp. 38–39; © NHPA/Anthony Bannister, p. 41 (top).

Front Cover: © Jana Leon/Stone+/Getty Images.